PILT (Payments in Lieu of Taxes): Somewhat Simplified

M. Lynne Corn
Specialist in Natural Resources Policy

July 25, 2012

Congressional Research Service
7-5700
www.crs.gov
RL31392

CRS Report for Congress
Prepared for Members and Committees of Congress

Summary

Under federal law, local governments are compensated through various programs for reductions to their property tax bases due to the presence of most federally owned land. These lands cannot be taxed, but may create demand for services such as fire protection, police cooperation, or simply longer roads to skirt the federal property. Some of these programs are run by specific agencies and apply only to that agency's land. The most widely applicable program, administered by the Department of the Interior (DOI), applies to many types of federally owned land, and is called "Payments in Lieu of Taxes," or PILT. The authorized level of PILT payments is calculated under a complex formula. This report addresses only the PILT program administered by DOI. There is no PILT-like program generally applicable to military lands, but a small fraction of military lands are eligible for the DOI PILT program. Furthermore, PILT does not apply to Indian-owned lands, virtually none of which are subject to local taxes.

This report explains PILT payments, with an analysis of the five major factors affecting the calculation of a payment to a given county. It also describes the effects of certain changes in PILT in 2008. Previously, annual appropriations were necessary to fund PILT, but a 2008 provision (in P.L. 110-343) for mandatory spending ensured that, beginning with FY2008 and continuing through the payment to be made in 2012, all counties will receive 100% of the authorized payment. On July 6, 2012, the President signed P.L. 112-141, containing a provision extending mandatory spending to FY2013.

Other issues have been the inclusion of additional lands under the PILT program, particularly some or all Indian lands, which are not now eligible for PILT. Most categories of Indian-owned lands cannot be taxed by local governments, though they generally enjoy county services. In some counties, this means a very substantial portion of the land is not taxable. The remaining tax burden (for roads, schools, fire and police protection, etc.) therefore falls more heavily on other property owners. To help compensate for this burden, some counties have proposed that Indian lands (variously defined) be included among those eligible for PILT payments. Examples of other lands mentioned from time to time for inclusion are those of the National Aeronautics and Space Administration, and the Departments of Defense and Homeland Security. In addition, some counties would like to revisit the compensation formula to emphasize a payment rate more similar to property tax rates (which vary widely among counties), a feature that would be a major change in counties with high property values. Finally, for lands in the National Wildlife Refuge System (NWRS), some have argued that all lands of the system should be eligible for PILT, rather than limiting the PILT payments to lands reserved from the public domain and excluding PILT payments for acquired lands. The exclusion of NWRS-acquired lands affects primarily counties in eastern states.

With the extension of mandatory spending to FY2013, the program would return to funding through annual appropriations in FY2014. Over the next few years, the larger debate for Congress might then be summarized as three decisions: (1) whether to approve future extensions of mandatory spending (either temporary or permanent); (2) whether to make the diametrically opposed choice of reducing the program through appropriations or changing the PILT formula; and (3) whether to add or subtract any lands to the list of those now eligible for PILT payments. Background on all three issues is discussed here.

Congressional Research Service

Contents

Introduction 1
Changes to PILT in the 110th and 112th Congresses 4
How PILT Works: Five Steps to Calculate Payment 4
    Step 1. How Many Acres of Eligible Lands Are There? 4
    Step 2. What Is the Population in the County? 6
    Step 3. Are There Prior-Year Payments from Other Federal Agencies? 7
    Step 4. Does the State Have Pass-Through Laws? 8
    Step 5. What Is This Year's Consumer Price Index? 9
Putting It All Together: Calculating a County's Payment 10
    National Totals 12
From Authorization to Appropriation 12
Current Issues 12
    Inclusion of Indian Lands 13
    Inclusion of Urban Lands and Tax Equivalency 14
    National Wildlife Refuge System Lands 14
Congressional Interest 15

Figures

Figure 1. Total PILT Payments, FY1993-FY2012: Appropriations in Current and
    Inflation-Adjusted Dollars (to 2010) 2
Figure 2. Total PILT Payments, FY1993-FY2012 Authorized Amount and Appropriation 3
Figure 3. Ceiling Payments Based on County Population Level, FY2012 7
Figure 4. PILT Payment Level as a Function of Specific Prior Payments (FY2012) 8
Figure 5. Steps in Calculating PILT for Eligible Federal Lands 11

Tables

Table 1. PILT Payments to Selected Urban Counties, FY2012 14
Table 2. NWRS Acres Eligible for PILT in Selected States, FY2010 15
Table A-1. Total PILT Payments, FY1993-FY2012: Appropriations in Current and
    Inflation-Adjusted Dollars (to 2010) 16
Table A-2. Total PILT Payments, FY1993-FY2012, Authorized Amount and
    Appropriation 17
Table A-3. Prior-Year Payment Laws That Are Offset Under Next PILT Payment 18

Appendixes
Appendix. PILT Data Tables 16

Contacts
Author Contact Information 20

Introduction

Generally, federal lands may not be taxed by state or local governments unless the governments are authorized to do so by Congress. Because local governments are often financed by property or sales taxes, this inability to tax the property values or products derived from the federal lands may affect local tax bases, sometimes significantly. Instead of authorizing taxation, Congress has usually chosen to create various payment programs designed to compensate for lost tax revenue. These programs take various forms. Many pertain to the lands of a particular agency (e.g., the National Forest System or the National Wildlife Refuge System).[1] The most wide-ranging payment program is called "Payments in Lieu of Taxes" or PILT.[2] It is administered by the Department of the Interior and affects most acreage under federal ownership. Exceptions include most military lands and lands under the Department of Energy (DOE lands have their own smaller payment program).[3] In FY2012, the PILT program covered 606.5 million acres, or about 94% of all federal land.

The Payments in Lieu of Taxes Act of 1976 (P.L. 94-565, as amended, 31 U.S.C. §§6901-6907) was passed at a time when U.S. policy was shifting from one of disposal of federal lands to one of retention. The policy meant that the retained lands would no longer be expected to enter the local tax base at some later date. Because of that shift, Congress agreed with recommendations of a federal commission that if these federal lands were never to become part of the local tax base, some compensation should be offered to local governments to make up for the presence of non-taxable land within their jurisdictions.[4] Moreover, there was a long-standing concern that some federal lands produced large revenues for local governments, while other federal lands produced little or none. Many Members, especially those from western states with a high percentage of federal lands, felt that the imbalance needed to be addressed. The resulting law authorizes federal PILT payments to local governments that may be used for any governmental purpose.

Many of the issues addressed when PILT was created have continued. One issue is the appropriate payment level, complicated by later erosion of the purchasing power of the payments due to inflation. For many years, counties held that payments were effectively declining because of inflation. Then PILT was amended in 1994. The authorized payment level went up (adjusted annually for inflation), but continued to be subject to annual appropriations. **Figure 1** shows a major increase in the actual and inflation-adjusted dollars appropriated for PILT from FY1993 to

---

[1] For more information on some of these agency-specific payment programs, see CRS Report RL30335, *Federal Land Management Agencies' Mandatory Spending Authorities*, by M. Lynne Corn and Carol Hardy Vincent; and CRS Report R41303, *Reauthorizing the Secure Rural Schools and Community Self-Determination Act of 2000*, by M. Lynne Corn. The program under the Department of Energy is described in U.S. General Accounting Office [now Government Accountability Office], *Energy Management: Payments in Lieu of Taxes for DOE Property May Need to Be Reassessed*, GAO/RCED-94-204 (Washington, DC: July 1994).

[2] U.S. Department of the Interior, Office of Budget, *Payments in Lieu of Taxes: National Summary Fiscal Year 2012*, Washington, DC, 2012. A similar document is issued every year; each contains tables for payments and acreage by state and county. To query data from the most recent fiscal year, see http://www.doi.gov/pilt/.

[3] A program, commonly referred to as Impact Aid, supports local schools based on the presence of children of federal employees, including military dependents. It provides some support to local governments, however, and to some extent it compensates for lost property tax revenue when military families live on federally owned land. For more information, see CRS Report RL33960, *The Elementary and Secondary Education Act, as Amended by the No Child Left Behind Act: A Primer*, by Rebecca R. Skinner.

[4] Public Land Law Review Commission, *One third of the Nation's Land: A Report to the President and to the Congress*, Washington, DC, June 1970, pp. 235-241.

FY2012.[5] But the 1994 amendments, designed to overcome years of erosion due to inflation, caused the authorized payment level to increase still faster. (See **Figure 2**.)

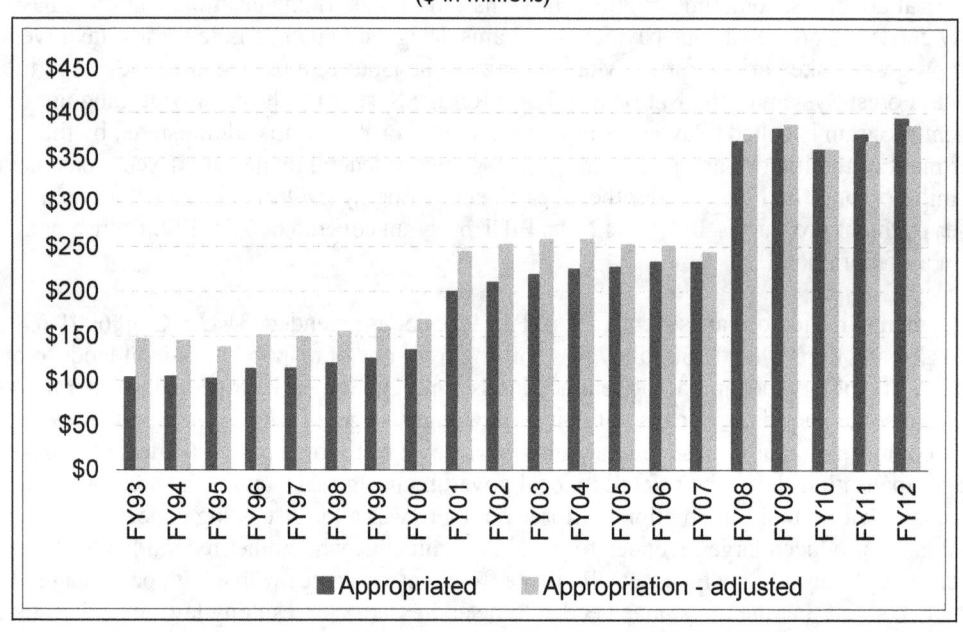

Figure 1. Total PILT Payments, FY1993-FY2012: Appropriations in Current and Inflation-Adjusted Dollars (to 2010)
($ in millions)

Source: Current dollars from annual *Payments in Lieu of Taxes: National Summary*. Inflation adjustment is based on chain-type price index.

Note: For the same data in tabular format, see **Table A-1**.

Critics of PILT cite examples of what they view as its "quirkiness." First, while there is no distinction between acquired and public domain lands[6] for other categories of eligible lands, acquired lands of the Fish and Wildlife Service (FWS) are not eligible for PILT—to the consternation of many counties in the East and Midwest, where nearly all FWS lands were acquired. Second, while payments under the Secure Rural Schools (SRS) program[7] require an offset in the following year's PILT payment for certain lands under the jurisdiction of the Forest Service, if the eligible lands are under the jurisdiction of the Bureau of Land Management (BLM), no reduction in the next year's PILT payment occurs.[8] Third, while payments under the Bankhead-Jones Farm Tenant Act (7 U.S.C. §1012) require a reduction in the following year's PILT payment if the lands are under BLM, no such reduction occurs if Bankhead-Jones payments are for lands under the Forest Service. Fourth, some of the "units of general local government"[9]

---

[5] Inflation adjustments in this report use the implicit price deflator for the Gross Domestic Product. See http://faq.bea.gov/cgi-bin/bea.cfg/php/enduser/std_adp.php?p_faqid=513.

[6] *Acquired lands* are those which the United States obtained from a state or individual. *Public domain lands* are generally those which the United States obtained from a sovereign nation.

[7] See CRS Report R41303, *Reauthorizing the Secure Rural Schools and Community Self-Determination Act of 2000*, by M. Lynne Corn.

[8] All of the BLM lands eligible for SRS payments are in Oregon.

[9] *Unit of general local government* is defined in the law (31 U.S.C. §6901(2)) as "a county (or parish), township, (continued...)

that receive large payments have other substantial sources of revenue, while some of the counties receiving little are relatively poor. Fifth, a few counties which receive very large payments from other federal revenue-sharing programs (because of valuable timber, mining, recreation, and other land uses) nonetheless are also authorized to receive a minimum payment ($0.34 per acre)[10] from PILT, thus somewhat cancelling out the goal of evening payments across counties. Sixth, in some counties the PILT payment greatly exceeds the amount that the county would receive if the land were taxed at fair market value, while in others it is much less. Given such issues, and the complexity of federal land management policies, consensus on substantive change in the PILT law has been elusive, particularly when Congress has a stated goal of reducing federal expenditures.

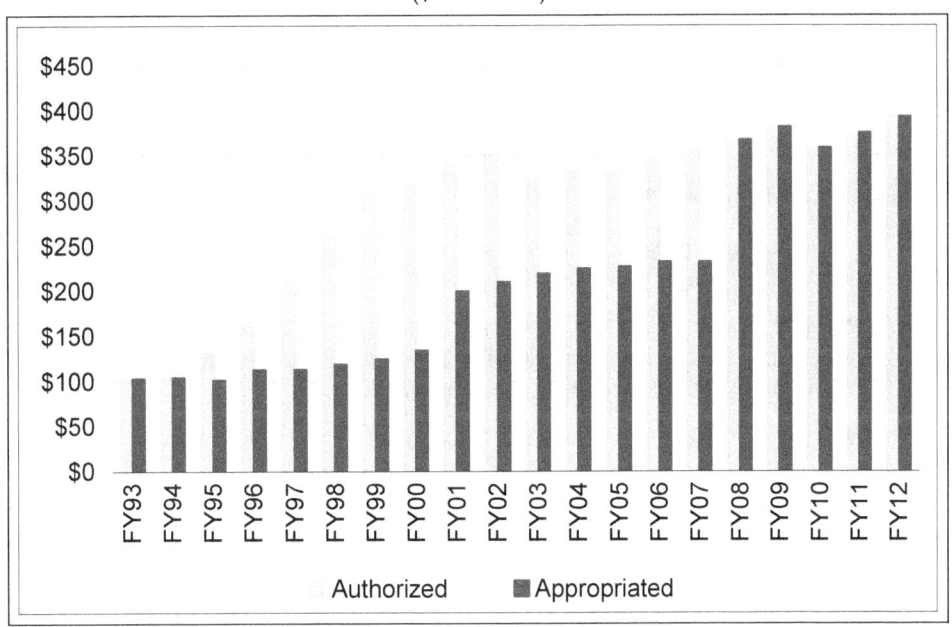

Figure 2. Total PILT Payments, FY1993-FY2012 Authorized Amount and Appropriation
($ in millions)

Source: Annual Payments in Lieu of Taxes: National Summary.
Note: For the same data in tabular format, see **Table A-2**.

(...continued)
borough, or city where the city is independent of any other unit of general local government, that (i) is within the class or classes of such political subdivisions in a State that the Secretary of the Interior, in his discretion, determines to be the principal provider or providers of governmental services within the State; and (ii) is a unit of general government as determined by the Secretary of the Interior on the basis of the same principles as were used on January 1, 1983, by the Secretary of Commerce for general statistical purposes" plus the District of Columbia, Puerto Rico, Guam, and the Virgin Islands. To avoid the use of the unwieldy *unit of general local government*, the word *county* will be used in the rest of this report, and must be understood here to be equivalent to the above definition. This shorthand is often used by DOI.

[10] This and subsequent references to payment rates and ceilings are based on FY2012 figures unless otherwise noted.

Changes to PILT in the 110th and 112th Congresses

The Continuing Appropriations Act, 2009 (P.L. 110-329), provided the FY2008 level ($228.9 million) through March 6, 2009; if this had been the full-year appropriation, it would have constituted roughly 61% of the figure estimated for full payment of the FY2009 authorized level. However, Section 601(c) of Title VI of P.L. 110-343 (the Emergency Economic Stabilization Act of 2008) provided for mandatory spending of the full authorized level for five years—FY2008-FY2012. For FY2008, an additional payment was made to raise the FY2008 level to the full authorized amount, and for FY2009-FY2012, the payments are at 100% of the authorized amount. On July 6, 2012, the President signed P.L. 112-141, whose Section 100111 extends mandatory spending for PILT to FY2013, without making any other changes to the law.[11]

How PILT Works: Five Steps to Calculate Payment

Calculating a particular county's PILT payment first requires answering several questions:

1. How many acres of eligible lands are in the county?
2. What is the population of the county?
3. What were the *previous* year's payments, if any, for all of the eligible lands under the other payment programs of federal agencies?[12]
4. Does the state have any laws requiring the payments from other federal agencies to be passed through to other local government entities, such as school districts, rather than staying with the county government?
5. What was the increase in the Consumer Price Index during the year?

Each of these questions will be discussed below. Finally, their use in the computation of each county's payment is described.

Step 1. How Many Acres of Eligible Lands Are There?

Nine categories of federal lands are identified in the law as eligible for PILT payments:[13]

1. lands in the National Park System;
2. lands in the National Forest System;

---

[11] As final agreement was being reached on this bill, the House Appropriations Committee reported H.R. 6091, which also extended PILT through FY2013. In light of the enactment of P.L. 112-141, the PILT provision of H.R. 6091 could be dropped at a later stage of its House or Senate consideration.

[12] Regardless of how many agencies have jurisdiction over eligible lands in a county, all of the payments specified in 31 U.S.C. §6903(a)(1) are added together and deducted from the following year's single PILT payment. Any other federal lands payments the county may get that are not specified in that provision are not deducted. The formula in 31 U.S.C. §6903 sets a cap on the total PILT payment for all of the eligible land in the county.

[13] See 31 U.S.C. §6901. The law refers to these nine categories of lands as "entitlement lands," and the term is used throughout the act. However, because *entitlement* is a word which is used in a very different, and potentially confusing, context in the congressional budget process, these lands will be called *eligible lands* in this report.

3. lands administered by the Bureau of Land Management;
4. lands in the National Wildlife Refuge System that are withdrawn from the public domain;
5. lands dedicated to the use of federal water resources development projects;[14]
6. dredge disposal areas under the jurisdiction of the U.S. Army Corps of Engineers;
7. lands located in the vicinity of Purgatory River Canyon and Piñon Canyon, Colorado, that were acquired after December 31, 1981, to expand the Fort Carson military reservation;
8. lands on which are located semi-active or inactive Army installations used for mobilization and for reserve component training; and
9. certain lands acquired by DOI or the Department of Agriculture under the Southern Nevada Public Land Management Act (P.L. 105-263).

Section 6904/6905 Payments

Two sections of the PILT law (31 U.S.C. §6904 and §6905) provide special payments for limited categories of land, for limited periods. These are described in the FY2012 *Payments in Lieu of Taxes: National Summary* (p. 12) as follows:

> Section 6904 of the Act authorizes payments for lands or interests therein, which were acquired after December 31, 1970, as additions to the National Park System or National Forest Wilderness Areas. To receive a PILT payment, these lands must have been subject to local real property taxes within the five year period preceding acquisition by the Federal government. Payments under this section are made in addition to payments under Section 6902. They are based on one percent of the fair market value of the lands at the time of acquisition, but may not exceed the amount of real property taxes assessed and levied on the property during the last full fiscal year before the fiscal year in which [they were] acquired. Section 6904 payments for each acquisition are to be made annually for five years following acquisition, unless otherwise mandated by law....
>
> Section 6905 of the Act authorizes payments for any lands or interests in land owned by the Government in the Redwood National Park or acquired in the Lake Tahoe Basin under the Act of December 23, 1980 (P.L. 96-586, 94 Stat. 3383). Section 6905 payments continue until the total amount paid equals 5 percent of the fair market value of the lands at the time of acquisition. However, the payment for each year cannot exceed the actual property taxes assessed and levied on the property during the last full fiscal year before the fiscal year in which the property was acquired by the Federal government.

In the FY2012 payments, the Section 6904/6905 payments totaled $609,568 or 0.16% of the total program. California counties received the largest amount ($107,846). Sixteen states and territories had no counties receiving payments under these two sections in FY2012. These states and territories were Alabama, Connecticut, Delaware, Illinois, Iowa, Kansas, New Jersey, North Dakota, Oklahoma, Rhode Island, South Dakota, Utah, Vermont, and Guam, Puerto Rico, and the Virgin Islands.

The payments under Section 6904 cease five years after acquired land is incorporated into a national park unit or a National Forest Wilderness Area. As a result, counties experience a sudden drop in their PILT payment after five years.

---

[14] These lands are under the jurisdiction of the Bureau of Reclamation, for the most part.

In addition, if any lands in the above categories were exempt from real estate taxes at the time they were acquired by the United States, those lands are not eligible for PILT, except in three circumstances:

1. land received by the state or county from a private party for donation to the federal government within eight years of the original donation;
2. lands acquired by the state or county in exchange for land that was eligible for PILT; or
3. lands in Utah acquired by the United States if the lands were eligible for a payment in lieu of taxes program from the state of Utah.

Only the nine categories of lands (plus the three exceptions) on this list are eligible for PILT payments; other federal lands—such as military bases, post offices, federal office buildings, and the like—are not eligible for PILT. The exclusion of lands in the National Wildlife Refuge System that are acquired is an interesting anomaly, and may reflect nothing more than the House and Senate committee jurisdictions at the time P.L. 94-565 was enacted.[15]

Step 2. What Is the Population in the County?

The law restricts the payment a county may receive based on population. Under the schedule provided in 31 U.S.C. §6903, counties are paid at a rate that varies with the population; counties with low populations are paid at a high rate per person, and populous counties are paid less per person. For example, for FY2012, a county with a population of 1,000 people will not receive a PILT payment over $166,210 ($166.21 per person); a jurisdiction with a population of 30,000 will not receive a payment over $2,493,900 ($83.13 per person). And no county is credited with a population over 50,000. Consequently, in FY2012, at the authorized payment level of $66.49 per person, no county may receive a PILT payment over $3,324,500 (50,000 x $66.49/person) regardless of population. **Figure 3** shows the relationship between the population of a county and the maximum PILT payment.

---

[15] At the time, jurisdiction over the National Wildlife Refuge System (NWRS) generally was in one committee, while jurisdiction over public domain lands was within the jurisdiction of a different committees. This was true in both the House and Senate. The committees considering PILT had no jurisdiction over the acquired lands within the NWRS.

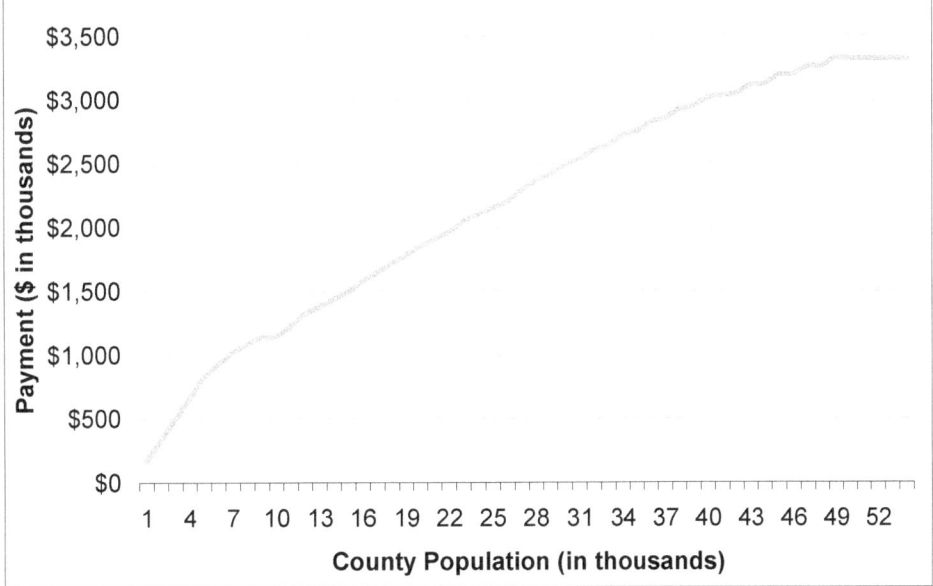

Figure 3. Ceiling Payments Based on County Population Level, FY2012

Source: Calculations based on *Payments in Lieu of Taxes: National Summary FY2012*, p. 14.

Step 3. Are There Prior-Year Payments from Other Federal Agencies?

Federal land varies greatly in revenue production. Some lands have a large volume of timber sales, some have recreation concessions such as ski resorts, and some generate no revenue at all. Some federal lands have payment programs for state or local governments, and these may vary markedly from year to year. To even out the payments among counties and prevent grossly disparate payments, Congress provided that the previous year's payments on eligible federal lands from specific payment programs to counties would be subtracted from the PILT payment of the following year. So for a hypothetical county with three categories of eligible federal land, one paying the county $1,000, the second $2,000, and the third $3,000, then $6,000 would be subtracted from the following year's PILT payment. Most counties are paid under this offset provision, which is called the *standard rate*. In **Figure 4**, the standard rate is shown by the sloping portion of the line, indicating that as the sum of the payment rates from other agencies increases, the PILT payment rate declines on a dollar-for-dollar basis.

Figure 4. PILT Payment Level as a Function of Specific Prior Payments (FY2012)

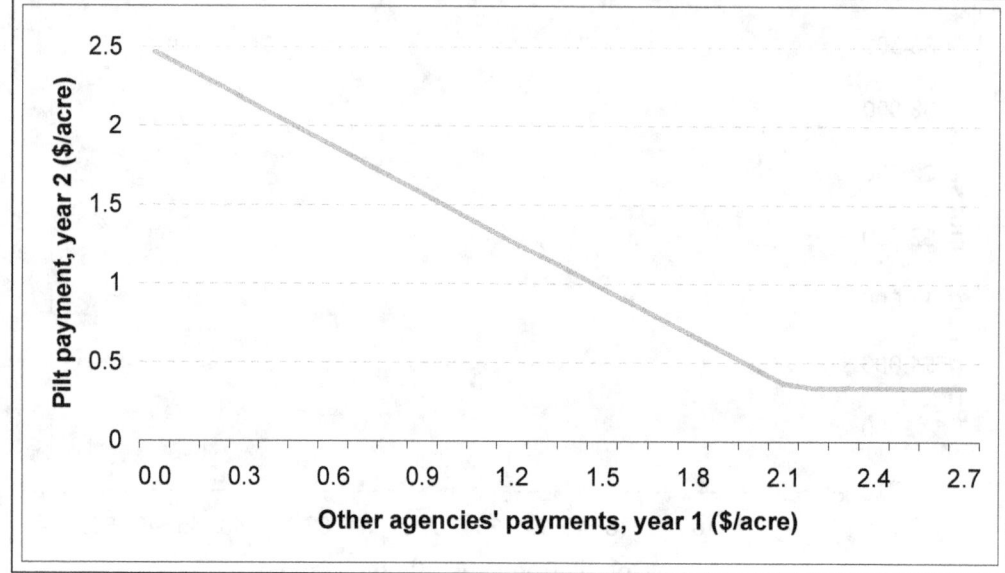

At the same time, Congress wanted to ensure that each county got *some* PILT payment, however small, even if the eligible lands produced a substantial county payment from other agencies. If the county had payments from three federal payment programs of $1,000, $2,000, and $1 million, for instance, subtracting $1.003 million from a small PILT payment would produce a negative number—meaning no PILT payment to the county at all. In that case, a *minimum rate* applies, which does not deduct the other agencies' payments. In **Figure 4**, the flat portion to the right shows that, after the other agencies' payments reach a certain level ($2.47 per acre in FY2012), the rate of the PILT payment remains fixed (at $0.34 per acre in FY2012).

The payments made in prior years that count against future PILT payments are specified in law (16 U.S.C. §6903(a)(1)). Any other payment programs beyond those specified would not affect later PILT payments. These specified payments are shown in **Table A-3**. Eligible lands under some agencies (e.g., National Park Service and Army Corps of Engineers) have no payment programs that affect later PILT payments.

Step 4. Does the State Have Pass-Through Laws?

Counties may receive payments above the calculated amount described above, depending on state law. Specifically, states may require that the payments from federal land agencies pass through the county government to some other entity (typically a local school district), rather than accrue to the county government itself. When counties in a "pass-through" state are paid under the formula which deducts their prior year payments from other agencies (e.g., from the Refuge Revenue Sharing Fund (RRSF; 16 U.S.C. §715s) of FWS, or the Forest Service (FS) Payments to States (16 U.S.C. §500)[16]), the amount paid to the other entity is *not* deducted from the county's PILT payments in the following year. According to DOI:

---

[16] Under 16 U.S.C. §500, these payments are made to the states or territories, and must be used for schools or roads in the counties where the national forests are located. Each state has its own rules on the mechanics of that transfer, on the proportion to be used for roads and the proportion for schools. Some states direct that the education portion be given (continued...)

Only the amount of Federal land payments actually received by units of government in the prior fiscal year are deducted. If a unit receives a Federal land payment, but is required by State law to pass all or part of it to financially and politically independent school districts, or any other single or special purpose district, payments are considered to have not been received by the unit of local government and are not deducted from the Section 6902 payment.[17]

For example, if a state requires all counties to pass along some or all of their RRSF payments from FWS to the local school boards, the amount passed along is not deducted from the counties' PILT payments for the following year (31 U.S.C. §6907). Or if two counties of equal population in two states each received $2,000 under the FS Payments to States, and State #1 pays that amount directly to the local school board, but State #2 does not, then under this provision, the PILT payment to the county in State #1 will not be reduced in the following year, but that of the county in State #2 will drop by $2,000. State #1 will have increased the total revenue coming to the state and to each county by taking advantage of this feature.[18]

Consequently, the feature of PILT that was apparently intended to even out payments among counties (at least of equal population size) may not have that result if the state takes advantage of this pass-through feature.[19] Under 31 U.S.C. §6903(b)(2), each governor gives the Secretary of the Interior an annual statement of the amounts actually paid to each county government under the relevant federal payment laws. DOI checks each governor's report against the records of the payment programs of federal agencies.

In addition, there is a pass-through option for the PILT payment itself. A state may require that the PILT payment itself go to a smaller unit of government, contained within the county (typically a school district) (16 U.S.C. §6907). If so, one check is sent by the federal government to the state for distribution by the state to these smaller units of government. The distribution must occur within 30 days. As of FY2012, Wisconsin is the only state to have selected this feature of PILT.

Step 5. What Is This Year's Consumer Price Index?

A provision in the 1994 amendments to PILT adjusts the authorization levels for inflation. The standard and minimum rates, as well as the payment ceilings, are adjusted each year. Under 31 U.S.C. §6903(d), "the Secretary of the Interior shall adjust each dollar amount specified in subsections (b) and (c) to reflect changes in the Consumer Price Index published by the Bureau of Labor Statistics of the Department of Labor, for the 12 months ending the preceding June 30." This is an unusual degree of inflation adjustment; no other federal land agency's payment program has this feature. But as will be shown below, increases in the authorization do not necessarily lead to a commensurate increase in the funds received by the counties.

(...continued)

directly to school boards. For more information see CRS Congressional Distribution Memo, *Forest Service Revenue-Sharing Payments: Distribution System*, by Ross W. Gorte, Nov. 19, 1999.

[17] U.S. Dept. of the Interior, *Payments in Lieu of Taxes: National Summary, Fiscal Year 2012*, p. 10.

[18] Note that even though a county as a whole may benefit from this provision, the county government *itself* will not, because it forgoes the revenues given directly to its school system.

[19] However, the Supreme Court has held that states cannot direct counties to spend their PILT payments (i.e., payments under the DOI-managed program described in this report) for particular purposes, once they have actually received their PILT payment. *Lawrence County v. Lead-Deadwood School District*, 469 U.S. 256 (1985).

Putting It All Together: Calculating a County's Payment

Knowing the answers to these questions, one can then make two comparisons to calculate the authorized payment level for a county. (**Figure 5** shows a flow chart of the steps in these comparisons.) All charts and comparisons in this report are based on FY2012 payment levels.

Alternative A. Which is *less*: the county's eligible acreage times $2.47 per acre or the county's ceiling payment based on its population? Pick the lesser of these two numbers. From it, subtract the previous year's total payments for these eligible lands under specific payment or revenue-sharing programs of the federal agencies that control the eligible land.[20] The amount to be deducted is based on an annual report from the governor of each state to DOI. This option is called the *standard provision*.

Alternative B. Which is *less*: the county's eligible acreage times $0.34 per acre or the county's ceiling payment? Pick the lesser of these two. This option is called the *minimum provision*, and is used in the counties that received relatively large payments (over $2.13 per acre for FY2012) from other federal agencies in the previous year.

The county is authorized to receive whichever of the above calculations—(A) or (B)—is *greater*. This calculation must be made for all counties individually to determine the national authorization level. From the program's inception through FY2007, the authorized payments were subject to annual appropriations, and if appropriations were insufficient for full funding, each county received a pro rata share of the appropriation. After passage of P.L. 110-343 and P.L. 112-141, each county receives the full authorized amount for FY2008-FY2013.

The combination of specific payments and PILT in the standard option means that reductions (or increases) in those other payments in the previous year could be exactly offset by increases (or reductions) in PILT payments. However, provided that the county's population is not so low as to affect the outcome, PILT payments cannot fall below $0.34 per acre for FY2012 (see Alternative B, above), so the full offset occurs only when the other federal payments in the previous year total less than $2.13 per acre (i.e., the maximum payment of $2.47 per acre minus the $0.34 per acre minimum payment from PILT).[21]

---

[20] Payments under the Secure Rural Schools program for Forest Service lands (but not Bureau of Land Management lands) are included among those prior year payments to be deducted. See CRS Report R41303, *Reauthorizing the Secure Rural Schools and Community Self-Determination Act of 2000*, by M. Lynne Corn.

[21] To illustrate more concretely, imagine each county as a large bucket, whose sides are marked off in "$/acre." PILT, in effect, checks the payment already in the bucket from other agencies, then adds at least enough money to the bucket to bring it to the $2.47/acre mark. Moreover, if the bucket is already above the $2.13/acre mark, PILT adds 34¢/acre, regardless of the amount in the bucket already. The money bucket could reach levels of $15/acre or more, with the last 34¢ added by PILT. The county population ceilings might then be thought of as holes in the sides of some of the buckets that prevent the buckets from filling beyond a certain level for that bucket (i.e., county).

Figure 5. Steps in Calculating PILT for Eligible Federal Lands
(FY2012 payment levels)

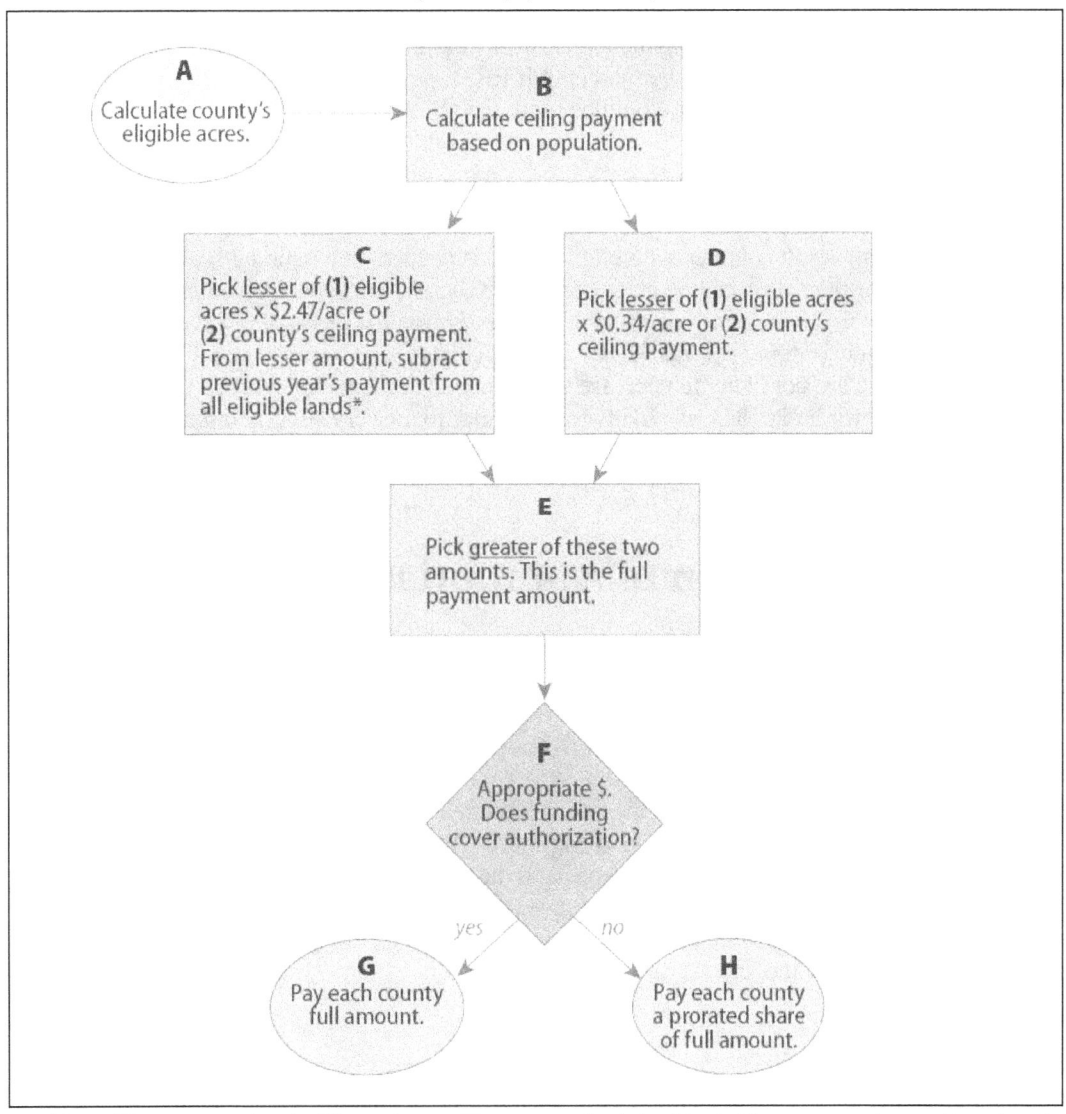

Note: The payments (marked *) are the specific payments for federal lands. The amount subtracted is reduced in states with pass-through laws. Also, funding covers authorization through FY2013; under current law, the PILT program returns to annual appropriations in FY2014.

Source: Prepared by CRS, based on PILT statute (31 U.S.C §§6901-6907).

The standard option, with its offset between agency-specific payments and PILT payments, still does not guarantee a constant level of federal payments to counties, because of the time lag in determining PILT payments. Federal payments for a given fiscal year are generally based on the receipts of the prior year. PILT payments of the *following* fiscal year are offset by these payments.

To illustrate, consider a county whose only eligible federal lands are under the jurisdiction of FWS. If the federal receipts on the FWS lands drop in FY2012 (compared to FY2011), payments in FY2013 from the FWS Refuge Revenue Sharing Fund will fall. PILT payments will therefore increase to offset the drop—in FY2013. (This example assumes that the PILT payment is calculated under the standard option.) The counties will be authorized to receive at least $2.47 per acre from RRSF and PILT payments combined,[22] but the two payments would not come in the same year. Consequently, if RRSF payments fall from year to year, the combined payments in the given year would be less than $2.47 per acre, but if RRSF payments rise, the authorized combined payment in the given year would be more than $2.47 per acre.

National Totals

Information from all 1,850 counties with eligible land is needed on a national scale before an aggregate figure for the nation can be calculated precisely, and consequently *no precise dollar figure can be given in advance for each year's PILT authorization level*.[23] However, because the amount for full authorization for FY2012 has been calculated, and because major changes in the factors stated above are not likely to decrease the payments at the national level, the full authorization level for FY2013 seems likely to be similar to, or very slightly larger than, the amount for the full authorization in FY2012 ($393.0 million), even though individual counties' payments may vary.

From Authorization to Appropriation

Until about 1994, the full amount authorized under the law's formula had generally been appropriated, with a few exceptions such as sequestration under the Gramm-Rudman-Hollings Act (Title II of P.L. 99-177). But the buying power of the payments fell due to inflation. In response, Congress amended the law in 1994 (P.L. 103-397) to adjust for inflation.

The amendment focused on increasing the total payments, building in inflation protection, and making certain additional categories of land eligible.[24] After the amendments passed, the increasing discrepancy between appropriations and the rapidly rising authorization levels led to even greater levels of frustration among local governments, and prompted intense interest among some Members in increasing appropriations. The result was the passage of P.L. 110-343 and P.L. 112-141. (See **Figure 2**, above.)

Current Issues

While the enactment of six years of mandatory spending put the issue of full funding to rest for the time being, in all likelihood county governments will strongly support continuing mandatory

---

[22] An exception would occur if the county's population is so small that the county is affected by the PILT ceiling on payments due to population.

[23] DOI does not include estimated full payment levels in its annual budget justification to Congress, and confines itself to the Administration's request for the year. However, DOI's annual report of current year PILT payments to counties includes this information.

[24] Other important issues in 1994 were the question of the equity of the payments and the balance struck in the payment formula (a) between heavily and sparsely populated communities, (b) between those with federal lands generating large revenues and those with lands generating little or no revenue, and (c) between the amounts paid under PILT and the amounts that would be paid if the lands were simply taxed at fair market value. But these issues were not addressed in the 1994 amendments and have scarcely been mentioned in the debate since then.

spending for PILT. This question has been the biggest issue facing the program in the 112th Congress. At the same time, with the congressional debate over spending levels in general, there may be proposals to modify or even eliminate PILT in later years as a means of reducing federal deficits. Three more specific issues are also being debated: inclusion of Indian or other categories of lands; tax equivalency, especially for eligible urban lands; and payments affecting the National Wildlife Refuge System.

Inclusion of Indian Lands

While the inclusion of other lands (e.g., military lands generally or those of specific agencies such as the National Aeronautics and Space Administration) under the PILT program has been mentioned from time to time, some counties with many acres of non-taxable Indian lands within their boundaries have long supported adding Indian lands to the list of lands eligible for PILT. The primary arguments made are that these lands receive benefits from the county, such as road networks, but Indian residents do not pay for them with property taxes; on the other hand, the federal government does not actually own these lands.

The complexity of the PILT formula makes it very difficult to calculate the consequences of such a move, either for authorization levels or appropriation levels. Additionally, Congress would have to decide what sorts of "Indian lands" would be eligible for such payments and a variety of other complex issues.[25] If some categories of Indian lands were to be added to those lands already eligible, Congress might wish to limit payments to counties with more than some minimum percentage of Indian lands within their borders. Regardless, even a very restrictive definition of "Indian lands" seems likely to add many millions of acres to those already eligible. Even if the criteria for eligibility were determined, it would still be difficult to determine the effect on authorization levels. To paint an extreme example, if all of the eligible Indian lands were in counties whose PILT payments were already capped due to the population ceiling, inclusion of Indian lands would have no effect on PILT authorization levels.

As long as mandatory spending is in place, appropriations would go up to fund the newly eligible lands. If mandatory spending expires and annual appropriations are less than the authorized level, each county would receive a pro rata share of the authorized full payment level. Individual counties whose eligible acres had jumped markedly with the inclusion of Indian lands might receive substantially more than in the past. Other counties (particularly those with few or no eligible Indian acres) would receive a smaller fraction of the authorized amount as limited dollars would be distributed among more lands.

---

[25] The many classifications of "Indian lands" include trust lands, restricted lands, and fee (private) lands, both on and off reservations. *Trust lands* are lands held by the federal government in trust for an Indian tribe or individual. *Restricted lands* are lands held by an Indian tribe or individual but subject to federal restrictions on alienation (e.g., sale) or encumbrance (e.g., mortgaging). Most, but by no means all, Indian trust and restricted lands are on Indian reservations. Trust and restricted lands, whether on or off reservations, are not subject to state or local land taxes. *On*-reservation Indian fee lands may or may not be subject to state and local land taxes, depending on the federal statute under which the land was fee-patented. *Off*-reservation Indian fee lands are generally subject to state and local land taxes. (Indian reservations may also include non-Indian fee lands, which are subject to state and local taxation.) Alaskan Native corporation lands (none of which are trust lands) are affected by the Alaska Native Claims Settlement Act's limits on state taxation. Congress would have to decide which of these many classifications of Indian lands would be subject to PILT benefits. Further, Congress might choose to distinguish between Indian lands which have never been taxed by a county or state versus those Indian lands that were once taxable but which were acquired into non-taxable status after some specified date.

Inclusion of Urban Lands and Tax Equivalency

Some observers have wondered whether urban federal lands are included in the PILT program. The response is that urban lands are not *excluded* from PILT under the current law. For example, in FY2012, the counties in which Sacramento, Chicago, and Cleveland are found, as well as the District of Columbia, all received PILT payments (see **Table 1**), though the property tax on similar, but non-federal, lands would likely have been substantially greater.

Table 1. PILT Payments to Selected Urban Counties, FY2012

County	Eligible Acres	FY2012 Authorized Payment ($)
Sacramento County (CA)	9,621	23,740
Cook County (IL)	139	343
Cuyahoga County (OH)	2,592	8,166
Arlington County (VA)	27	0[a]
District of Columbia	6,959	17,339

a. Under the formula, Arlington County's 27 eligible acres (all under the National Park Service) would generate a payment of $65. However, under the law, no payment is made for amounts under $100.

Source: U.S. Dept. of the Interior, *Payments in Lieu of Taxes: National Summary*, FY2012.

Eastern counties, which tend to be small, rarely have large populations *and* large eligible acreage in the same county. On the other hand, western counties tend to be very large and may have many eligible acres, and some, like Sacramento, may have large populations as well. Furthermore, as the cases of Arlington County and the District of Columbia illustrate, PILT payments are by no means acting as an equivalent to property tax payments, because if the 6,959 acres in the District of Columbia or the 27 acres in Arlington County were owned by taxable entities, those entities would surely pay much more than $17,339, or $0, respectively, in property taxes.

Because the formula in PILT does not reflect an amount commensurate with property taxes, counties such as these might support a revised formula that would approach property tax payments.

National Wildlife Refuge System Lands

As noted above, lands in the National Wildlife Refuge System (NWRS) that were withdrawn from the public domain are eligible for PILT, and those that were acquired are not. In addition, the National Wildlife Refuge Fund (NWRF, also called the Refuge Revenue-Sharing Fund, or RRSF) relies on annual appropriations for full funding. For FY2012, payments for NWRF are approximately 24% of the authorized level. For refuge lands eligible for PILT, some or perhaps all of the NWRF payment will be made up for in the following year's PILT payment, but for acquired lands, this will not occur because they are not eligible for PILT. Congress may consider making all refuge lands eligible for PILT, and/or providing mandatory spending for NWRF, as it has for PILT. Eastern counties could be the largest beneficiaries of such a change, although some western states may also have many NWRS acres that are not currently eligible for PILT. (See **Table 2** for selected state examples.) Adding the 10.9 million acres of NWRS lands currently ineligible for PILT would increase PILT lands by 1.8%.

Table 2. NWRS Acres Eligible for PILT in Selected States, FY2010

State	NWRS Acres Reserved from Public Domain	Total NWRS Acres	Percent Eligible for PILT
Alabama	0	71,386	0.0
Arizona	1,553,465	1,740,545	89.2
Iowa	334	118,473	0.3
Maine	0	68,107	0.0
Montana	433,135	1,445,163	30.0
Ohio	77	9,234	0.8
Oregon	275,018	590,741	46.5

Source: *Annual Report of Lands Under Control of the U.S. Fish and Wildlife Service As of September 30, 2010* (the most recent year available).

Congressional Interest

Congressional interest, after the 1994 revisions to PILT, has focused on the three areas cited above: (1) whether to approve mandatory spending (either temporary or permanent); (2) whether to make the diametrically opposed choice of reducing the program through appropriations or through changing the PILT formula; and (3) whether to add or subtract any lands to the list of those now eligible for PILT payments. PILT payments for FY2012 totaled $393.0 million in mandatory spending; in contrast, the annual appropriation contained in P.L. 112-74 for the bulk of funding for the Department of the Interior was $10.3 billion, or 26 times the PILT program. For a relatively small fraction of the federal budget, PILT garners considerable attention for local reasons: (1) according to the FY2012 *Payments in Lieu of Taxes: National Summary*, 1850 counties were eligible for PILT; (2) the average payment per county (many of which are sparsely populated) was $212,456; (3) while some counties received only $100 (below which figure PILT makes no payment), many received over $1 million and 14 received over $3 million.[26] The resulting impact on budgets of local governments helps generate interest despite the comparatively small size of the PILT program.

---

[26] *Payments in Lieu of Taxes: National Summary*, FY2012. The 14 counties were in seven states: AK (1), AZ (3), CA (3), NV (2), NM (1), UT (2), and WY (2).

Appendix. PILT Data Tables

The first two tables below show the data presented in **Figure 1** and **Figure 2**. The third shows the agency payments that offset payments under PILT in the following year.

Table A-1. Total PILT Payments, FY1993-FY2012: Appropriations in Current and Inflation-Adjusted Dollars (to 2010)

($ in millions)

Year	Appropriation	Inflation-Adjusted Appropriation
1993	103.2	146.31
1994	104.1	144.54
1995	101.1	137.51
1996	112.8	150.55
1997	113.1	148.33
1998	118.8	154.07
1999	124.6	159.25
2000	134.0	167.63
2001	199.2	243.69
2002	209.4	252.09
2003	218.6	257.75
2004	224.7	257.68
2005	226.8	251.73
2006	232.5	249.98
2007	232.5	242.93
2008	367.2	375.35
2009	381.6	385.99
2010	358.1	358.10
2011	375.2	375.16
2012	393.0	384.79

Source: Current dollars from annual *Payments in Lieu of Taxes: National Summary*. Inflation adjustment is based on chain-type price index.

Notes: For the same data in a bar chart, see **Figure 1**.

Table A-2. Total PILT Payments, FY1993-FY2012, Authorized Amount and Appropriation

($ in millions)

Year	Authorized	Appropriated
1993	103.2	103.2
1994	104.4	104.1
1995	130.5	101.1
1996	165.1	112.8
1997	212.0	113.1
1998	260.5	118.8
1999	303.7	124.6
2000	317.6	134.0
2001	338.6	199.2
2002	350.8	209.4
2003	324.1	218.6
2004	331.3	224.7
2005	332.0	226.8
2006	344.4	232.5
2007	358.3	232.5
2008	367.2	367.2
2009	381.6	381.6
2010	358.1	358.1
2011	375.2	375.2
2012	393.0	393.0

Source: Annual *Payments in Lieu of Taxes: National Summary.*

Notes: For the same data in a bar chart, see **Figure 2**.

Table A-3. Prior-Year Payment Laws That Are Offset Under Next PILT Payment

Federal Agency Making Payment	Short Title of Law or Common Name	P.L. or Date	U.S. Stat.	U.S. Code	Lands Eligible for Payments	Payment Rate
Forest Service	"25% payments" or "Payments to states"	Act of May 23, 1908 (ch. 192, §13)	35 Stat. 260	16 U.S.C. §500	All NF lands	25% of gross receipts to state for roads and schools in counties
	None	Act of June 20, 1910 (ch. 310)	36 Stat. 557, §6	not codified	NF lands in AZ and NM	Proportion of lands in National Forests (NFs) reserved for schools times proceeds from sales in NF
	None	Act of June 22, 1948 (ch. 593, §5); Act of June 22, 1956 (ch. 425, §2)	62 Stat. 570, 70 Stat. 328	16 U.S.C. §577g, §577g-1	Lands in Superior NF, MN	0.75% of appraised value (in addition to 25% payments above)[a]
	Mineral Leasing Act for Acquired Lands (§6)	Act of Aug. 7, 1947	61 Stat. 915	30 U.S.C. §355	NF lands with mineral leasing	50% of mineral leasing revenues to states for counties
	Material Disposal Act	Act of July 31, 1947 (§3)	61 Stat. 681	30 U.S.C. §603	Net revenues from sale of land and materials	Varies depending on type of receipt and agency
	Secure Rural Schools and Community Self-Determination Act[b]	P.L. 106-393, as amended	114 Stat. 1607, as amended	16 U.S.C. §7101 et seq.	NF lands (but not lands under Land Utilization Program (LUP) or National Grasslands), if this option is chosen by county instead of 25% payments	Complex formula, see CRS Report R41303, *Reauthorizing the Secure Rural Schools and Community Self-Determination Act of 2000*
Bureau of Land Management	Mineral Lands Leasing Act	Act of February 25, 1920 (ch. 85, §35)	41 Stat. 450	30 U.S.C. §191	Public lands	50% of leasing revenues to states for counties
	Taylor Grazing Act	Act of June 28, 1934 (ch. 865, §10)	48 Stat. 1273	43 U.S.C. §315i	Public lands	12.5% of grazing receipts to states for counties
	Bankhead-Jones Farm Tenant Act	Act of July 22, 1937 (ch. 513, §33)	50 Stat. 526	7 U.S.C. §1012	National Grasslands and LUP lands managed by BLM	25% of revenues for use of lands to states

Federal Agency Making Payment	Short Title of Law or Common Name	P.L. or Date	U.S. Stat.	U.S. Code	Lands Eligible for Payments	Payment Rate
	Mineral Leasing Act for Acquired Lands (§6)	Act of Aug. 7, 1949	61 Stat. 915	30 U.S.C. §355	Public lands with mineral leasing	50% of mineral leasing revenues to states for counties
	Material Disposal Act	Act of July 31, 1947 (§3)	61 Stat. 681	30 U.S.C. §603	Net revenues from sale of land and materials	Varies depending on type of receipt and agency
Fish and Wildlife Service	Refuge Revenue Sharing Act	Act of June 15, 1935 (ch. 261, §401(c)(2))	49 Stat. 383	16 U.S.C. §715s(c)(2)	Public domain lands in NWRSc	25% of net receipts from timber, grazing, and mineral sales directly to county; remaining 75% to counties under other formulas
Federal Energy Regulatory Commission	Federal Power Act	Act of June 10, 1920, (ch. 285, §17)	41 Stat. 1072	16 U.S.C. §810	NF and public lands with occupancy and use for power projects	37.5% of revenues from licenses for occupancy & use to states for counties

Sources: 31 U.S.C. §6903(a)(1), *Payments in Lieu of Taxes: National Summary FY2012*, p. 13. The latter document has typographical errors which are corrected here, as noted. Because the various payment laws are identified in some documents by title, in others by a U.S. Code citation, or still others by the Statutes at Large, or date, or Public Law, all of these are cited here, where they exist.

a. *Payments in Lieu of Taxes: National Summary FY2012* erroneously states payment rate is 75% of appraised value.

b. When payments are made for lands under the jurisdiction of the Forest Service for the Secure Rural Schools (SRS) program, the payments result in a reduction (offset) in the following year's PILT payment. However, if the lands are under BLM jurisdiction, no offset is made in the following year's PILT payment. All BLM lands eligible for SRS payments are in Oregon.

c. Acquired lands in the National Wildlife Refuge System are not eligible for PILT payments. See text.

Author Contact Information

M. Lynne Corn
Specialist in Natural Resources Policy
lcorn@crs.loc.gov, 7-7267